HOLIDAY FAVORITES

Solos and Band Arrangements
Correlated with Essential Elements® Band Method

Arranged by ROBERT LONGFIELD, JOHNNIE VINSON, MICHAEL SWEENEY *and* PAUL LAVENDER

Welcome to Essential Elements Holiday Favorites! There are two versions of each selection in this versatile book. The SOLO version appears in the beginning of each student book. The FULL BAND arrangement of each song follows. The ONLINE RECORDINGS or PIANO ACCOMPANIMENT BOOK may be used as an accompaniment for solo performance. Use these recordings when playing solos for friends and family.

PLAYBACK+
Speed • Pitch • Balance • Loop

To access audio visit:
www.halleonard.com/mylibrary

Enter Code
4282-9922-9614-8533

ISBN 978-1-5400-2785-6

HAL•LEONARD®

00870004

Visit Hal Leonard Online at
www.halleonard.com

Contact Us:
Hal Leonard
7777 West Bluemound Road
Milwaukee, WI 53213
Email: info@halleonard.com

In Europe contact:
Hal Leonard Europe Limited
42 Wigmore Street
Marylebone, London, W1U 2RN
Email: info@halleonardeurope.com

In Australia contact:
Hal Leonard Australia Pty. Ltd.
4 Lentara Court
Cheltenham, Victoria, 3192 Australia
Email: info@halleonard.com.au

AULD LANG SYNE

FLUTE
Solo

Words by ROBERT BURNS
Traditional Scottish Melody
Arranged by MICHAEL SWEENEY

00870004

FELIZ NAVIDAD

FLUTE
Solo

Music and Lyrics by
JOSÉ FELICIANO
Arranged by PAUL LAVENDER

PARADE OF THE WOODEN SOLDIERS

FLUTE
Solo

English Lyrics by BALLARD MacDONALD
Music by LEON JESSEL
Arranged by PAUL LAVENDER

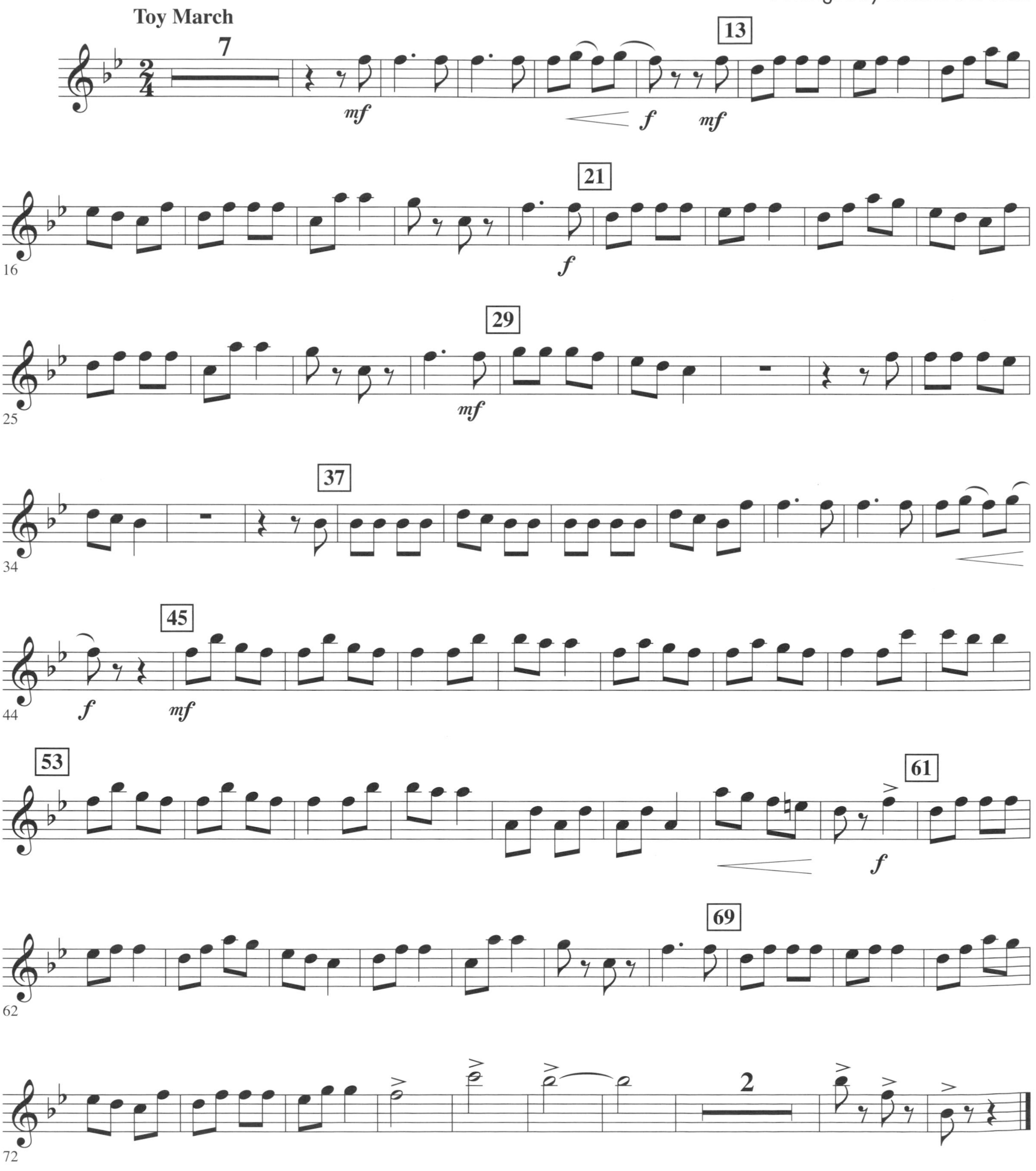

GOOD KING WENCESLAS

FLUTE
Solo

Words by JOHN M. NEALE
Music from PIAE CANTIONES
Arranged by ROBERT LONGFIELD

00870004

PAT-A-PAN
(Willie, Take Your Little Drum)

FLUTE
Solo

Words and Music by
BERNARD de la MONNOYE
Arranged by ROBERT LONGFIELD

SILVER BELLS

FLUTE
Solo

Words and Music by
JAY LIVINGSTON and RAY EVANS
Arranged by PAUL LAVENDER

00870004

DO YOU HEAR WHAT I HEAR

FLUTE
Solo

Words and Music by
NOEL REGNEY and GLORIA SHAYNE
Arranged by MICHAEL SWEENEY

From THE SOUND OF MUSIC

MY FAVORITE THINGS

FLUTE
Solo

Lyrics by OSCAR HAMMERSTEIN II
Music by RICHARD RODGERS
Arranged by ROBERT LONGFIELD

00870004

From the Motion Picture Irving Berlin's HOLIDAY INN

WHITE CHRISTMAS

FLUTE
Solo

Words and Music by
IRVING BERLIN
Arranged by JOHNNIE VINSON

CHRISTMAS TIME IS HERE

FLUTE
Solo

Words by LEE MENDELSON
Music by VINCE GUARALDI
Arranged by JOHNNIE VINSON

00870004

From Warner Bros. Pictures' THE POLAR EXPRESS

THE POLAR EXPRESS

FLUTE
Solo

Words and Music by
GLEN BALLARD and ALAN SILVESTRI
Arranged by JOHNNIE VINSON

AULD LANG SYNE

FLUTE
Band Arrangement

Words by ROBERT BURNS
Traditional Scottish Melody
Arranged by MICHAEL SWEENEY

FELIZ NAVIDAD

FLUTE
Band Arrangement

Music and Lyrics by
JOSÉ FELICIANO
Arranged by PAUL LAVENDER

00870004

PARADE OF THE WOODEN SOLDIERS

FLUTE
Band Arrangement

English Lyrics by BALLARD MacDONALD
Music by LEON JESSEL
Arranged by PAUL LAVENDER

GOOD KING WENCESLAS

FLUTE
Band Arrangement

Words by JOHN M. NEALE
Music from PIAE CANTIONES
Arranged by ROBERT LONGFIELD

00870004

PAT-A-PAN
(Willie, Take Your Little Drum)

FLUTE
Band Arrangement

Words and Music by
BERNARD de la MONNOYE
Arranged by ROBERT LONGFIELD

SILVER BELLS

FLUTE
Band Arrangement

Words and Music by
JAY LIVINGSTON and RAY EVANS
Arranged by PAUL LAVENDER

00870004

DO YOU HEAR WHAT I HEAR

FLUTE
Band Arrangement

Words and Music by
NOEL REGNEY and GLORIA SHAYNE
Arranged by MICHAEL SWEENEY

From THE SOUND OF MUSIC

MY FAVORITE THINGS

FLUTE
Band Arrangement

Lyrics by OSCAR HAMMERSTEIN II
Music by RICHARD RODGERS
Arranged by ROBERT LONGFIELD

From the Motion Picture Irving Berlin's HOLIDAY INN

WHITE CHRISTMAS

FLUTE
Band Arrangement

Words and Music by
IRVING BERLIN
Arranged by JOHNNIE VINSON

00870004

CHRISTMAS TIME IS HERE

FLUTE
Band Arrangement

Words by LEE MENDELSON
Music by VINCE GUARALDI
Arranged by JOHNNIE VINSON

From Warner Bros. Pictures' THE POLAR EXPRESS

THE POLAR EXPRESS

FLUTE
Band Arrangement

Words and Music by
GLEN BALLARD and ALAN SILVESTRI
Arranged by JOHNNIE VINSON

00870004